SPEED READING
TECHNIQUES
COMPREHENSIVE GUIDE WITH
TIPS AND EXERCISES

Table of Contents

Introduction

Reading is an integral part of everyday life as everyone will be called to do some reading at least once a day. Whether that has to do with reading E-Mails, Newspapers, letters, books, advertisements, TV subtitles, live updates, product manuals or a text message or anything else, it is significant that one has a developed reading skill. Most people take that skill for granted but that should not be the case. As a matter of fact, reading is a skill that needs meticulous practice and constant training in order to be mastered. And mastering this skill is important so as to be a fast and efficient reader saving yourself time for other activities.

But who is an efficient reader?

In order to define the so-called "efficient" reading it's important to consider two things: a person's speed in combination with the necessary time to grasp the essence; to understand the content of a text. Speed is a skill that can be improved with constant practice and exercises. Any ordinary reader can improve the speed required to read a text and there are various techniques for doing so; turning an average reader into a speed reader. There is no doubt that devotion, consistency, and concentration are required for the mastering of this skill but it is worth the while as once done, one can read twice as fast than an average reader.

As research has shown, an average reader can read from 200 to 350 words per minute. With the appropriate techniques and practice, this speed can be raised from 500 to 600 words per minute. Those techniques that are anything but hard will be presented later on. What is important is that one can achieve the seemingly unrealistic reading speed of 800 to 900 words per minute through consistent practice and the efficient application of those speed reading techniques that will be discussed in the following chapters.

This book mainly focuses on speed reading techniques and tries to explain the most important concepts related to reading, the mental processes required, and the necessary brain-eye coordination. On top of that, it presents some tested and approved speed reading exercises for the readers. Those exercises intent to train an average reader into becoming a speed reader. There is no need to spend money on speed reading courses and classes- one can become a speed reader through consistent practice and by following the tips presented in this book.

The Reading Process

Before we start, it is crucial to understand the reading process. Daily everyone is called to read and does so without thinking the how or why. Only a few individuals bother to think about how one reads or how the eyes work or the mental processes required for reading. When we try to think about the reading process, we come to know that this for granted skill is a complex system of brain-eye coordination; our eyes are receivers of information and our brain is on the receiving end to decode the information provided by the eyes into a concept we are able to understand.

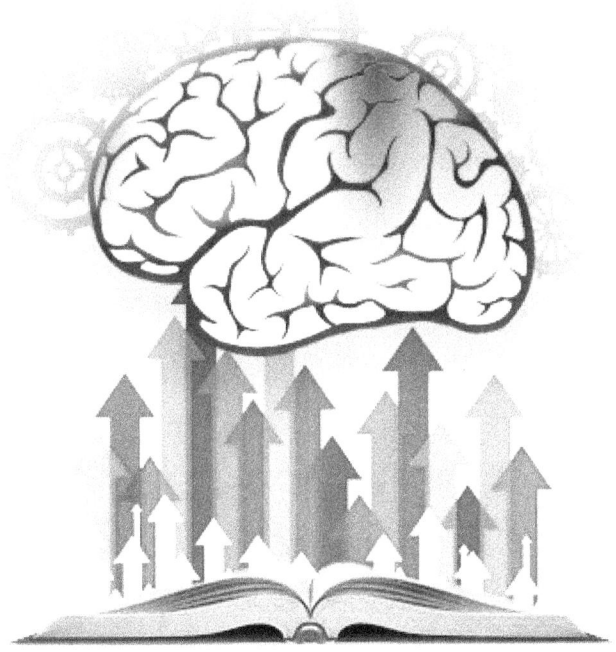

Conventionally, researchers believe that both eyes focus on specific letters while reading. However, recent researches reveal that this is not really the case as now scientists and opticians believe that each eye focuses on different letters at a given time (usually, a couple of letters apart in a given word). Let see what happens in practice.

Look at the words below:

Speed Reading Techniques

<u>What happens with your eyes? Where is your focus?</u>

When you read it, your eyes do not focus on each and every

letter.

They simply focus on the bold ones:

Speed **R**eading **T**echniqu**es**

Now, try to read the following phrase:

Speed **R**aednig **T**cehinqeus

While reading, the brain hardly notices the shuffling of letters, and we simply read it as 'Speed Reading Techniques", right? – Well, you will probably wonder why this happens. The answer is simple: the brain simply forms an image by processing the letters the eyes focus on and then it analyses the virtual image and determines the word. It is a lightening quick process, we don't really notice everything while we read.

That is as it is easier for the brain to detect the difference because now the letters in focus have been shuffled (note that in the previous phrase focused letters had not been shuffled and that caused the brain to read the assumed phrase). Now try reading the following sentence:

Seped Redeing Tecihnequs

What you will see is that as the bold letters have been misplaced, the brain easily detects the difference and takes a little time to determine the exact words.

Having seeing various situations that one might face when reading let's get to the scientific why.

Sub-Vocalization

Whether you believe it or not, every reader pronounces each word in his or her head while reading. This is called vocalization and there may be a difference of intensity of vocalization in each person but everyone forms this habit unconsciously. To justify this view, reading experts call this habit "Sub-Vocalization" and it is an important part of the reading process. It is a natural process according to which when a person reads a word, he or she virtually hears the word sound in mind. The drawback is that hearing takes a bit longer as compared to the time needed to understand the word (sight is always swift as compared to the sound or hearing).

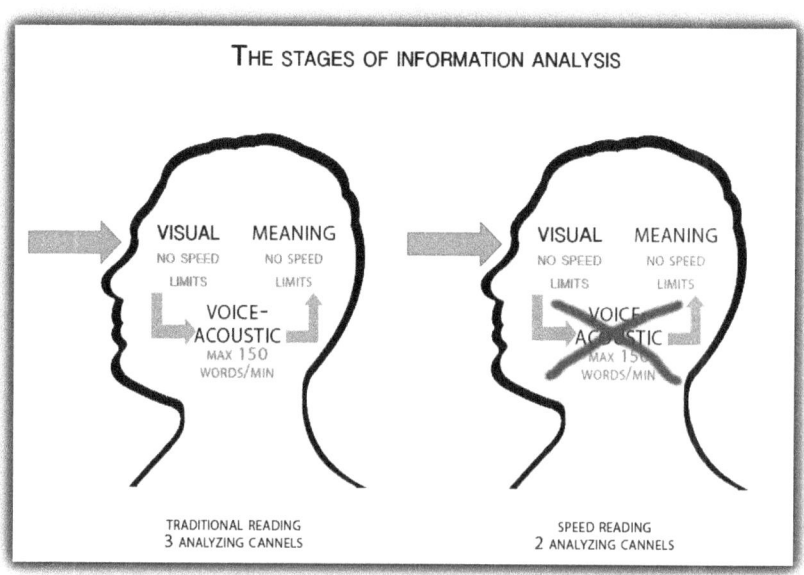

In order for one to become a speed reader, one needs to mute 'sub-vocalization' as it is a habit of procrastination holding the readers back. You must be wondering how is this possible – But it is. Only after realizing that sub-vocalization occurs while reading, it can be turned Off though practice and focus. Mostly, people try reading Word-Blocks to work around this habit. It is comparatively difficult to read Word-Blocks as compared to structured sentences. Despite of how hard this might seem, researchers claim that it is the most important phase of increasing the reading speed. If sub-vocalization is not turned down; it is virtually impossible to raise the reading speed up to 600+ words a minute.

Do you want to be a speed reader? If yes try to first acknowledge when you sub-vocalize and then once you start consciously noticing its occurrence, try reading without thinking or try word blocks. You might not make it at first but I'm telling you eventually will get read of this habit and maximize your potential to be a speed reader. What else happens though?

Concentrating on every word consumes additional time, and it is not an ideal way for efficient reading. That is as the focus shifts to discrete words rather than the meaning of the sentence.

An efficient reader adopts the 'chunking' technique, a technique which is based on reading multiple words in blocks. Not only reading word-by-word is time-consuming, but when you concentrate on separate words, you often miss the overall concept of what is being said. It is a fact that people who read each word as a distinct unit can understand less than those who read faster by "chunking" words together in blocks. That is why 'chunking' is the practice to be used in reading as the reader tries to increase the number of words in a word-block when reading. To expand on this, it is a good idea to keep the text away from the eyes. In this way, the word-block will automatically increase.

Eye Movement

Peripheral vision is what most of the readers fail to use efficiently. The human eye has the ability to span 1.5-inches at a given time which covers up to four or five words (depending on the font size). When peripheral vision is not used, the chances to see the corners words are eliminated. That is as peripheral vision depends upon the softening of the gaze and relaxing the face. The key is to avoid stressing the eyes to focus on distinct words and this is the most important tip for reading word-blocks.

Regression

Usually, the readers tend to re-read specific words or phrases. This practice is called regression. It is also called 'skipping back', and it wastes a lot of time.

What happens? What is regression?

People often tend to jump back a few lines to make sure that they have read something correctly. Be very conscious of regression, and don't allow yourself to re-read material unless you absolutely have to. A good habit that helps you focus is to run the finger or the pencil tip along the text you are reading. In such cases, the reading speed depends upon the speed of the pencil tip or the finger running along the text.

Lack of Concentration

Lack of concentration is a huge problem in every aspect of our lives including reading. While reading, this lack of concentration is usually caused by what we call multitasking. The best solution then to avoid this is to not do other things simultaneously with reading. Also, it is essential that the external environment does not distract the reader, and this is why the selection of a proper space or place is vital for speed reading. Having chosen that place where you can read without distractions it is now time to clear your head and think of nothing other of what you read as you don't want to be carried away by your personal thoughts and miss the point of what you read having to start the paragraph over.

Having explained all the necessary attitudes of a speed reader it is important to shed some light on the various **Misconceptions about Reading**. Those misconceptions refer to some urban myths that create confusion in peoples' minds when they are called to decide on whether or not they should speed read.

I.   Swift Reading Decreases Retention

It is generally believed that reading swiftly results in retention decrease. That is not actually the case as speed reading techniques are mostly devised in an attempt to improve the level of understanding while maintaining a fast reading speed.

II.   Linear Reading is a Must

Another popular misconception is that reading should be linear. However, research shows that it is not the hard and fast rule. There are cases when the writers themselves begin a book by writing the ending and then composing the plot based on that ending. Generally, this technique is practiced in story writing. For example, in the movies, the ending is foreshown at the beginning of the movie and the whole story moves back and forth as a stream of consciousness.

FACT

Reading faster +
comprehend better =
good reader

Good readers get
MORE pleasure and
meaning out of what
they read

III.   Thorough Reading is Vital for Better Understanding

In school, students have to follow the word by word technique when reading their textbooks but this habit changes as they grow older. Though, it is hard for them to get rid of this habit completely as they are not convinced that but word-by-word reading does not ensure a better understanding of the concept.

IV.   Reading is Natural

After all, reading is a natural process as language was created by humans (probably 15 million to 50 million years ago), yet the exact origin of language is still debatable. Linguists claim that the human race first used an alphabet almost 5000 years ago. Bearing in mind the time required for the physical evolution of a living thing, 5000 years is relatively less time for the human brain to turn into a language processing or a reading machine.

FACT

Sᴘᴇᴇᴅ READERS CLUMP WORDS INTO GROUPS

Sᴘᴇᴇᴅ READING IS ABOUT INCREASING VISUAL SPAN AND NOT FOCUSING ON EVERY SINGLE WORD – ONE AT A TIME

Some Important Statistics

The complexity of a text affects the reading speed as well as the understanding of its concept. This complexity might be the result of the advanced diction and the type of reading material (page or screen). Experts tend to rate readers by using the statistics displayed in the following table:

SCREEN	PAPER	COMPREHENSION	READER'S LEVEL
100 wpm	110 wpm	50%	Below Average
200 wpm	240 wpm	60%	Average
300 wpm	400 wpm	80%	Good
700 wpm	1000 wpm	85%	Excellent

Note: WPM refers to words per limit. So according to this table, an excellent reader should be able to read around 700 words per minute in screen, 1000 words per minute in paper and understand about 85 percent of what of the content.

AND YES that person CAN be YOU!

Speed Reading Benefits

So far what has analyzed is the reading process as well as the techniques required for Speed Reading. This chapter will discuss the benefits that one has when Speed Reading. Speed Reading is not an art that deals with fast reading, it is a skill for the improvement of the reader's comprehension ability. It is tied to the vitality of understanding the concepts set forth in the text. The main advantage of speed reading is that it enables the reader to gain much more knowledge in a given time as compared to an average reader.

Swift Understanding

The brain needs consistent training in order to perform well in time. Think about a video game with multiple stages. The human brain needs some time to get accustomed to the presented conditions. Similar is the case of the speed reading skill which is improved through different exercises; the level of understanding increases with practice and exercise. If carefully selected, speed reading exercises enable the reader to get the better understanding of the text without losing the speed.

Confidence

It is a usual case for people to judge another person when he or she starts to speak. Speed reading equips the reader with many assets in no time. It becomes easier for the speed reader to prepare for a meeting, discussion or a presentation if he or she is able to go through more written content as compared to the average reader. In this way, the speed reader remains in the comfort zone when it comes to sharing new ideas, facts, and information on any given topic. It casts a positive impact on the personality and also raises the level of confidence. Definitely, when one has read a lot about a certain topic, he or she will have enough information and logic to present while addressing an audience.

Sharp Memory

Speed reading sharpens the memory and the ability to retain facts and information. Memory is linked to the ability to comprehend and to an improved understanding ability, the brain acts efficiently to store facts in memory. Further, memory is one of the many determinants of creativity and it is sharp memory that leads to creativity.

Neuroplasticity

Neuroplasticity is related to the brain's ability to connect different concepts. It empowers the individual to integrate different concepts so as to have logical conclusions. Speed reading helps neuroplasticity of the human brain. It enables the speed reader to think better, make quick decisions, have logical conclusions, integrate the concepts and think out of the box. This quality enables the speed reader to stand out in professional life.

Improved Focus

Speed reading is what trains the reader to maintain focus on the text. Gradually, with the help of practice and consistency, the brain gets accustomed to focusing on the important task at hand rather than concentrating on distractions. Focus is graded as a high quality for the office workers. That is as lack of focus definitely, leads to mistakes and it poses a negative impact on the personality of an individual.

☐

Keys to Successful Speed Reading

There is a difference between knowing "HOW" to speed read and actually doing it. Theoretical knowledge is one thing but putting theory into practice in real life situations is altogether different. What follows is tested keys to becoming a successful speed reader:

- Never underestimate the importance of consistent practice. If you practice occasionally, you will never get your desired results. Practice and as much as you can follow it, a set schedule is the first key to successful speed reading.

- Train yourself gradually without trying to jump on to the difficult level from the start. It is important to realistically analyze your reading skills and then begin with the easy drill/exercises. The human brain better learns with a step-by-step practice starting from the easy drills and moving towards the tough ones only after mastering the easier stages.

- Never ignore the comprehension ability. People generally think that speed reading is all about reading rapidly. Always focus on the speed and the level of understanding of the concept. Reading words at a fast rate is not the ultimate goal. The main objective is to understand the text while reading at a fast pace.

- DO NOT try to speed read legal documents, confidential data, terms and policies, agreements and undertakings, etc. It is better to read them word-by-word by using sub-vocalization. Never forget to read such documents at least twice.

- Never forget to record your reading speed. In this way, you will be able to track the improvement in your reading skill as you jump from one level to the next, during the practice session.

In the next chapter we will have a look at the most important speed reading techniques to work with in order to become efficient speed readers.

Speed Reading Techniques

Keys to successful speed reading are important but they require some techniques to give desired results. One can only benefit from the keys to successful reading by practicing and implementing some important speed reading techniques. The important part is to know the purpose of each technique and then to try achieving that purpose. There is no doubt that one can improve his or her reading speed and comprehension to as much as 700 to 900 words per minute. But, before thinking about such an appealing statistic, do not forget that it requires consistent training and experimentally verified techniques. If you are wondering why so, you should know that there are is a big variety of techniques to become an efficient speed reader, but only the tested and credible set of techniques will provide results and those are the techniques that will be discussed here.

Before moving to the techniques, one must prepare for the perfect reading environment. Let us have a quick look at these preparatory steps:

- Determine the objective of reading in a particular text. You must ask yourself WHY you are reading this text. It could be a newspaper, magazine, novel, poetry or a letter. Be clear about the purpose of reading the specific text. It is important because once you know the objective only then you will be interested in reading it.

- Avoid all the possible distractions before you set yourself to read. Silence your phone. Clear your mind from external thoughts. Turn off the TV and chose a pin drop silent place. You can also ask others around to stay away for a while.
- Sit comfortably and begin from the title page. Never forget to read the text printed inside the cover. It will give a clear idea of what the book is all about.

Now it is the time to talk about the speed reading techniques one-by-one:

Use a Pointer

A pointer may be a pencil or fingertip. The function of the pointer is to guide the eye movement. What happens is that our brain orders the eyes to follow the moving object. When the pointer is moved along the text, the brain actually forces the eyes to follow this movement.

Note: Never try to move the pointer too fast in the beginning. Adjust the movement realistically depending on your current reading speed. Increase the pointer speed gradually during different phases of the practice session.

Apart from guiding the eye movement, the pointer performs another key function. It is difficult for most people to fix their eyes on the page. Even the smallest of distractions get the eyes away from the page. The pointer keeps the eyes focused on the page and restricts the brain from getting easily distracted.

Avoid Sub-Vocalization

We have already discussed the concept of sub-vocalization while explaining the reading process in detail. In short, it is the practice of hearing your sound in your mind when you read a word. Scientists have revealed that sub-vocalization is the result of a person's habit of reading aloud at the young age (usually in the school age). The brain gets accustomed to the word sounds, and it keeps sounding them even if you read in with complete silence.

Sub-Vocalization hinders speed reading. It is important to turn-off the mind's sound while reading. There is one highly credible technique to avoid sub-vocalization. It is simple yet effective; simply set the speed of the movement of the pointer a bit faster as compared to the speed at which your mind sounds the word. This simple tip is effective, but it takes some time to set it right. Do not get disappointed if you don't succeed immediately. Practice and focus will result in your favor.

Note: Never forget to acknowledge that the mind actually sounds the words you read. When you become conscious of this, only then you can turn it Off by moving the pointer a bit fast.

NEVER FORGET that speed reading is not all about reading at a quick pace. Always know the limits and try to improve gradually rather than being unrealistically optimistic.

Always remember the objective. But it does not mean to ignore the speed. The point is to keep an eye on the speed, record it during the practice session and note the progress. Once again the pointer speed comes into play. Researchers have revealed that through practice, the brain gets accustomed to the pointer speed. The key here is to control the pointer speed and not try to over-speed this rate of eye movement. The best determinant to figure out your potential speed is to notice at what speed you tend to get exhausted. As soon as your feel that you are getting exhausted, restrict the speed and make it a bit slower, once again by slowing down the speed of the pointer.

Note: You may speed the pointer up in case if a point is repeated just to remind the reader of something which he or she has already gone through. In this case, you can save time by skimming the pointer along the lines.

Retention refers to memorizing the important facts in the text. It is vital to keep in mind these important facts otherwise the purpose of reading will not be materialized. Sometimes, one has to slow down in order to concentrate on important sayings, dialogues, and facts and figures. It is suggested that the reader must develop the ability to control the reading speed. He or she must know where to skim, where to increase the reading speed and where to slow things down just to get a clear idea and to memorize important points.

Active Reading

The world record of speed reading is a remarkable fact. The world champion has set the record by reading 4,700 words in one minute.

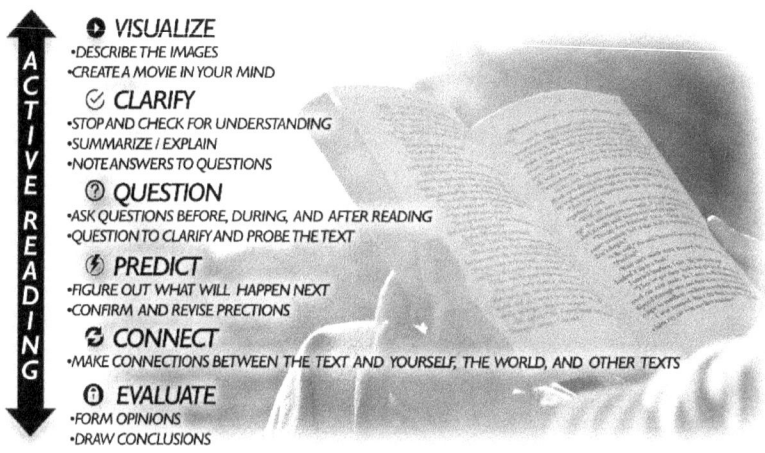

Believe it or not, this individual with an unbelievable reading speed can read a novel or a book in less than hour. Is this person able to retain what he reads at this speed? The fact is that the retention capacity starts to decrease as soon as the reading speed hits 1500 words a minute. This type of speed is only suitable if the text is fairly simple and written for entertainment purposes.

Most of the content we come across on a daily basis contains something that matters to us. Active reading becomes significant when it comes to such important content. Take the example of product manuals and guides. You cannot afford to read the manual at a rate of 1000 words per minute without clearly understanding the instructions. You cannot hand a pallet shooting airgun over to a teenager by asking him to go through the user guide quickly. So active reading becomes necessary in such cases where you cannot ignore neither facts nor instructions.

Consistency

Every skill requires consistent practice and so does the speed reading. The reader must be willing to focus, remain consistent and follow the set schedule for exercise or training. A non-serious attitude cannot get the reader to anticipated results. The human brain likes to perform when it is asked to do so regularly. You cannot expect the mind to perform brilliantly if the task at hand is practiced few and far between. Anybody who claims to increase your reading speed up to 1000 words per minute in one week is simply exaggerating. The human brain needs time so as to master any skill. It is not an electronic device equipped with built-in programming. What a human brain does best is what it repeatedly does. Consistency also means to keep practicing even when you reach the speed of 700 words per minute. If you quit reading after achieving a greater speed, your reading speed will decrease due to the absence of regular practice. So you can also say that to be a speed reader, in the long run, one must develop the habit of reading. One way of developing the habit of reading is to enjoy reading rather than taking it as an imposed activity.

Always LOVE Reading

This is one of the most important speed reading techniques. It also develops the habit of reading. Suppose if you do not like to read books and you are looking for something which could attract you towards reading then get ready.

First of all, think of your most favorite topic. It could be music, Hollywood, celebrities, relationships, history, art, mythical heroes and villains, etc. If you don't find your interest in these things, then we have something which will catch your attention. Think about your childhood years. Suppose they are from 1993 to 1998, simply search for the children story books from those years. Start reading, and you will LOVE reading these books over and over. Once you develop the habit of reading, only then you can practice speed reading exercises but bear in mind that It requires motivation and mental readiness. Don't think of it as a necessary evil but take it as a sweet companion in isolation.

Using the Eye Span

The drawback of reading word-by-word is that the eyes focus on the words being read. There is a simple tip for avoiding the lack of reading speed in this case. Remember that an average human eye has 1.5-iches wide span which covers four to five words. When reading a sentence, it is better for the eyes to focus on the middle words. For example, in a sentence that contains 10 words, the eyes' focus on the center words (4th and 5th) so that the left eye will cover the first five words and the right eye will cover the next five words.

In simple words, try to read the sentence in a single glance rather than focusing on the words one by one.

Speed Reading Exercises

Exercises are important to improve speed reading skills. The theory itself is not enough to master any skill. A practical orientation is the only thing which generates the desired results. Let us begin with the basic speed reading exercises for beginners:

Before starting these drills, please make sure to record your current reading speed.

Steps to Follow

I.   Select the reading material which you normally read

II. Read at your normal speed. Do not try to put extra effort in an attempt to read at a quick pace. Read for just 10 minutes. (Read for comprehension and understandability)

III. Note where you start reading and count the words after you read for about 10 minutes

IV. Take some time, relax and start reading the same text again. This time, try to read the specific text in less than 10 minutes. (You may set your personal target at 8 minutes)

V.   As you are reading the same text again, naturally, it will be easier for you to read it a bit quicker than the first time. (Do not forget the use of the pointer)

VI. Repeat this exercise again and this time try to read the text in 6 minutes (do not ignore comprehension)

VII.   Once, you manage to read the same text in 6 minutes, close the text. Find some new text and give it a go for 10 minutes. (do not choose a complicated text, try to keep the same type of text)

VIII.   Note the number of words you read in those 10 minutes. Hopefully, it will turn out to be an improved reading speed. Repeat the same exercise with this text as you did with the first text.

IX.   Invest at least one hour per day in this simple exercise.

Exercise for Eye-Movement

Eye movement is controlled by a muscular mechanism. It can be controlled and improved through regular drills. Here are some simple but effective eye-movement drills for the readers:

i.   Thumb-to-Thumb Glance

This simple drill improves peripheral vision. It will ultimately stretch the eye muscles resulting in an improved flexibility. Here is what you need to do:

a. Sit comfortably or stand still

b. Keep your head still (this is important)

c. Stretch your arms (30 degrees from your eyes, either side)

d. Position your hands, thumbs-up

e. Keeping the head still, glance between the thumbs, right to left and then left to right (Keep doing for at least 120 seconds)

f. Repeat the exercise five to four times (don't forget to take 2 minutes break between each drill)

ii.   Eye Writing

This exercise is good for the flexibility of the eyeballs. It increases the range of movement of the eyeballs.

a. Sit or stand still and look at the front wall in the room.

b. Think of a word in your mind.

c. Imagine that you are writing that word by using your eye movement.

d. Repeat the drill 10 to 15 times per day

iii.   Scattered Words

This exercise is simple yet effective. It is not only good for speed reading, but it also forces the eyes to push the limits for quick movement.

a.   Take a drawing chart

b.   Write 20 to 30 words (scattered)

c.   Paste or hang the chart on the front wall

d.   Take a stopwatch to note the time

e.   Start reading all the words

f.   Note the time taken for reading all the words

g.   Repeat the exercise 10 to 15 times

h.   Replace the chart and use the new one new words

i.   With the passage of time, try to include long and complex words

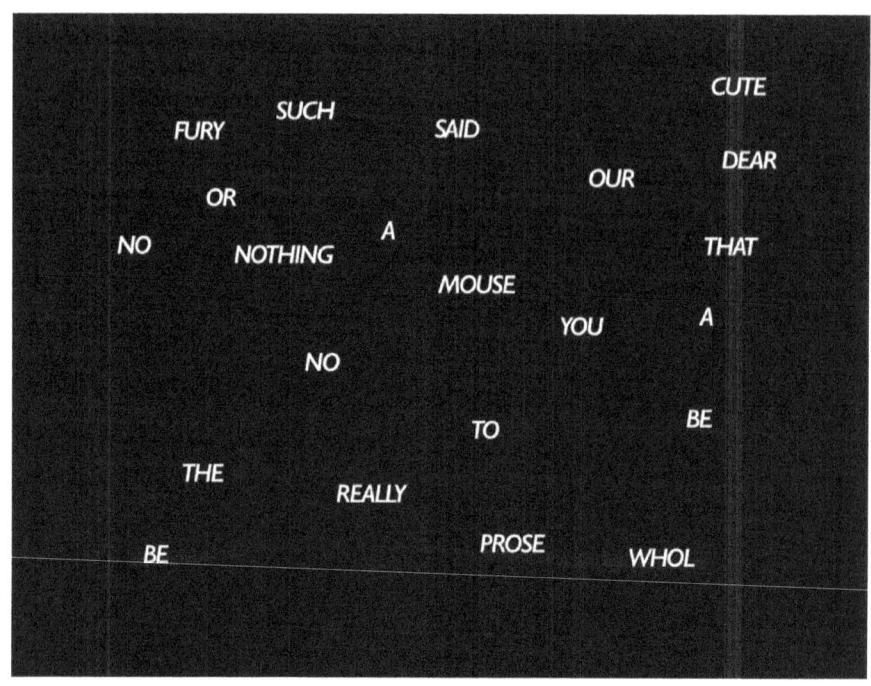

CUTE
FURY   SUCH   SAID
                              OUR   DEAR
    OR
NO   A   THAT
    NOTHING
              MOUSE
                        YOU   A
          NO

                    TO   BE
THE
          REALLY

BE   PROSE   WHOL

You can use any background color that suits your eyes.

road
saw
          trust
they doubt
              make
some
              goods
stone   said
              knot photo
blue
    award   lion

There is a simple exercise which is vital in order to strengthen your eyes while reading. Just follow the steps below:

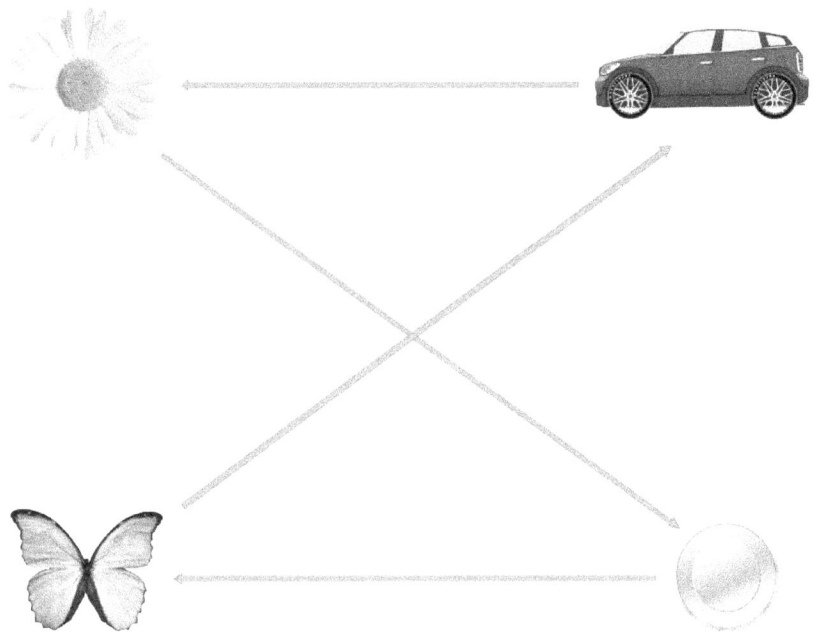

I.   Choose the starting point and set your eyes on it

II.   Move your eyes following the arrow directions

III.   Repeat it 10 to 15 times

Now in the next picture, notice that the objects are same, but the pattern has been changed. Repeat the above exercise with the next picture:

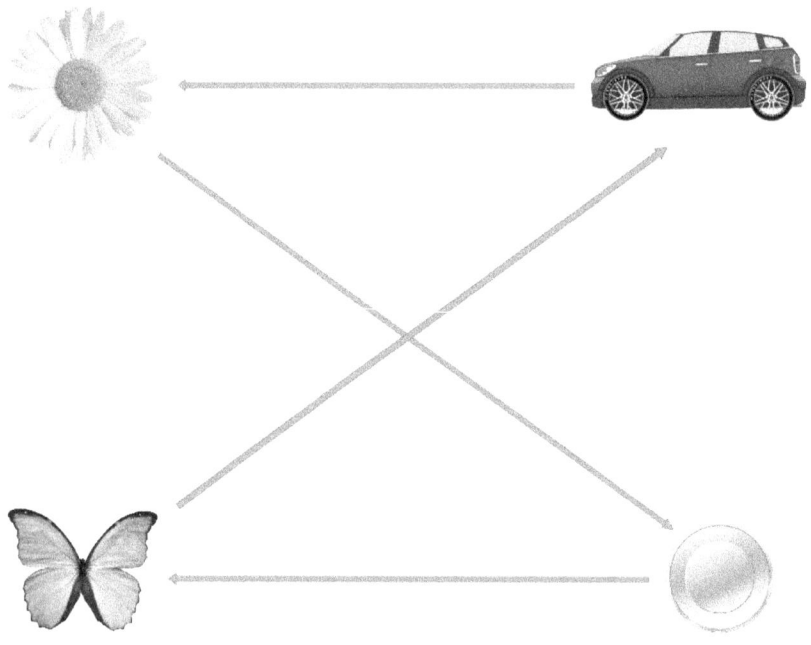

The View Vision Exercise

As previously discussed, speed readers don't read word by word; rather they take the whole paragraph as a single picture. At least they read 10 to 12 words (bulk reading) at a time.

Look at the following pictures. What you need to do is simply focus your eyes on the DOT in the center and try to read all the letters scattered around without moving your eyeballs.

Now try the same exercise on the following pattern:

Let's kick it up a notch. This time you need to keep the eyes focused in vertical line between the text and read the text without moving your eyes in any direction.

This

exercise

will help you

to expand your vision

span by working on your

peripheral vision. You can read

more words at a time when your vision span is wider

Now keep your eyes focused in the middle of the two pyramids and try to read the whole paragraph. It is important to read the whole paragraph as it contains the exercise technique.

In the next chapter, we will move on to Bill Cosby's speed reading techniques which hold a vital significance for better understanding and comprehension of the text.

The   two

stop   method

Invented by   Wade E Cutler

and the main technique   is to minimize the eye

movement. Instead of read   each word separately try

to look at every line twice only. First after the first third of the

line, and second after the third third. That speed reading exercise will

increase you reading speed and you eyes will not be exhausted. If you will keep

practice this method, you will be able to read full line without moving your eyes!

Believe me, it's possible!

Bill Cosby's Speed Reading Strategies

Practicing the exercises in the previous chapter is to accustom the eyes, brain and hands with the speed reading environment and settings. Speed reading strategies are focused on the preliminary orientation of the given text. These techniques are meant to ask some questions about the given text and to get a clear idea about the concept without wasting much time. When it comes to reading, you can't get something for nothing. All efforts that are needed to gain literary polish always starts with reading. Reading is a significant and essential skill as compared to writing, and the non-reading of certain things is the dependent choice of intellect as compared to reading.

"READ WITH A GOOD LIGHT— AND WITH AS FEW FRIENDS
AS POSSIBLE TO HELP YOU OUT. NO TV, NO MUSIC.
IT'LL HELP YOU CONCENTRATE BETTER—AND READ
FASTER."

When you talk about reading just like writing it is a craft that
needs certain techniques for its optimization to achieve better
outcomes. Besides a large number of tutorials and books,
there are still some important tips that you will never be able to

get from other sources, these are the three proven strategies that will help you in reading faster.

"LEARN TO READ FASTER AND YOU'LL HAVE TIME FOR A GOOD LAUGH WITH MARK TWAIN — END A GOOD CRY WITH WAR AND PEME."

Have A Preview

First of all, preview the reading material so as to see if it is too hard or too long. Previewing is one of the essential skills and it is the ultimate strategy for speed reading as it provides the reader with a general idea to about heavy reading such as a long newspaper or magazine article, non-fictional books, and business reports.

PREVIEW

- READ HEADLINES AND SUBTITLES
- LOOK AT PICTURES AND OTHER
  GRAPHICS; READ CAPTIONS
- SKIM SIDE BARS
- READ SECTION OUTLINE IN TEXTBOOKS
  AND ARTICLES

This preview will allow you to comprehend at least half of the text in a small period of time. For instance, you will be able to preview a long report about 100 pages within an hour. This preview will enable you to decide that which part of the report is giving you a closer look and where you can get your desired material.

Let's have a look at how to preview a document or an article:

First of all, read the two paragraphs of the article or the document that you have selected. Now, read the first sentence of every paragraph below and then read the last two paragraphs completely. This preview will not provide you with all the details contained in the article, but it will save you time by giving you an idea of what you should read and what you should not. This short previewing provides an overall and quick view of the long material that you have not read before.

If you have a short reading, then there is another technique too.

Skim It

If you have a very simple and short reading, then it's better to follow skim. Skimming is one of the best ways to gain an overview of the small reading, including sports, magazines and entertainment sections in the newspaper.

SKIMMING

- SKIMMING IS USED TO **QUICKLY** IDENTIFY THE **MAIN IDEAS** OF A TEXT.

- WHEN YOU READ THE NEWSPAPER, YOU'RE PROBABLY NOT READING IT WORD-BY-WORD, INSTEAD YOU RE SCANNING THE TEXT.

HELPFUL TIPS

After skimming a weekly magazine, you will be able to read all the sections in half the time. It is also a best way to review the material that you have already read.

Let's see how to skim:

First of all, consider that your eyes are like a magnet so you can force them to work quickly and move fast. Have a quick sweep across every line in the article and select some of the keywords in every line. Skimming is different for everyone and so, people perform it differently. When two people are skimming, it's not possible for them to pick up the same words after skimming the same paper, but they will both get a general idea of the type of the document.

Skimming enables the reader to get a simple and complete idea about the story from a few words and it is not time-consuming.

- SKIMMING AND SCANNING IS USED WHEN READING ALL TYPES OF DOCUMENTS.
- WE SKIM TO GET THE IDEA OF WHAT A DOCUMENT IS ABOUT AND TYPICALLY SKIM ALL DOCUMENTS BEFORE WE ACTUALLY BEGIN TO READ.
- AS WE SKIM, WE...
  - THINK ABOUT THE TOPIC
  - THINK ABOUT WHAT WE ALREADY KNOW ABOUT THE TOPIC
  - START TO GUESS OR ANTICIPATE THE DETAILS WE ARE GOING TO READ ABOUT.
- WE SCAN FOR SPECIFIC INFORMATION.
- WE WORK QUICKLY WHEN WE SKIM AND SCAN.

Till now, you have learned that skimming and previewing helps the reader in getting a general idea of the article or the document in a quick way. But none of these techniques commit to providing comprehension above 50 percent as they don't include the reading of the entire document with each and every word that it contains. As it's already mentioned that no one can get something in return for nothing when it's all about the game of reading. In order to get a complete understanding of all the content, faster, there is a third technique.

This technique is helpful in quick understanding with enhanced comprehension and speed. Most of the people try to read the entire sentence by looking at every word such as; My – sister – Nina – thinks – that – Halloween…

You might also follow this reading pattern when difficult words are encountered or when a few words possess some extra special meanings such as in Shakespeare plays or in some poems. This is fine in all these situations.

But, when it's all about reading faster, then reading word by word is a putrid way as it can reduce your speed significantly.

When you try the clustering of the words by creating the clustering train instead of using one by one-word method, you will be able to enhance your reading speed significantly. Many of the people think that clustering is a totally different way of looking into the things that we are reading.

I. **First Method**

To perform clustering, you have to train your eyes to look at all words in the form of clusters: three or more words at the first glance.

If you are looking to find clusters, you will not get it the first time, it needs continuous practice and before your eyes start forming clusters automatically.

First of all, select something that must be light for reading. Read the content as fast as it is possible for you. Try to concentrate on three or more words in one glance instead of a single word at one time. Now, re-read the content in your normal speed and find out the things you have missed while you were reading faster.

II.   **Second Method**

First of all, try to cluster and then re-read in order to find out the things that you have missed.

When you will be able to read in the form of cluster for the first time without missing so many words, you will know that you have gained more speed in reading. You can enhance it more by practicing each and every day for about fifteen minutes. If you do so, mastering this technique will only take you a week. Try not to be disappointed if it takes longer for your skills to develop. Clustering all the words requires practice and time.

Generic Tips for Speed Reading

When it comes to speed reading, there are some simple but significant tips that everyone must follow if they really want to enhance their reading speed. These tips will enable them to make the most out of it. You can learn these generic tips and apply them to methods and this is how you will be able to take your reading speed to the higher level. But, you have to be patient if you want to achieve the highest level as you will not be the master of these skills in one day. After the so many years of learning and reading from an early age, you must have developed specific habits and patterns to assimilate information and thus will take time to get rid of all these habits. Succeeding in this though is a matter of time and the hard work and discipline.

Read in the Blocks and Chunks

At an early age, we are taught about the making of chunk letters in a complete word and now at this stage, so as to increase the speed of reading, this process needs to be taken to the new level. At this new level, when starting the chunking of individual words in the multiple word block they have to be read as a whole.

These blocks of words can then further be chunked in the larger blocks of words and sentences and ultimately as one complete chunk of paragraph that you can comprehend and read within a single look. At first, this process could be a daunting task as you might not be familiar to it. But you must not forget that you learned chunking letters into words when you were a child and it was difficult at first but with your constant struggle and determination you finally learned to read words quickly. You can start the process of speed reading by simply reading two-word chunks at a single time. Once you are comfortable with such a reading method, you can jump to the higher one that will involve the reading of three words and then towards four-word chunks and so on. After a while, your brain will be adjusted to the process and you will observe a quick increase in your reading speed. After every progress, you will be moved towards a larger chunk and this is how your reading speed will be improved from 50% - 70%.

Sentence Scanning

This method supposes that first two, last two and three words of any sentence are not important in defining the meaning of the complete sentence. Therefore, you can skim over such words by simply not reading them. After doing so, you will be able to understand the meaning of the sentence. By utilizing this simple and easy method, you will be able to gain more speed in reading and you will see an improvement from 10% - 20%.

Have you seen any typewriter while working? If not, then it moves from left to right and when the page edge is reached, it pushes to the left again. A few people also use this method. Such people suffer from the so called "Typewriter's Reading Syndrome" as they move their head from right to left or left to right as if their book is stretched to the complete horizon. Are you aware of the fact that when you move your head, your reading speed is reduced? Therefore, it is recommended that while reading the page, try to rotate and move your eyes in back and forth position, otherwise you will not be able to gain anything. This method will accelerate your reading speed from 20% - 30%. This does not function as a limitation; there is another possibility that involves the acceleration of the reading speed by the incorporation of the peripheral vision. This peripheral vision allows you to look at more than one page in single view without moving your eyes from right to left. Moreover, the best and quick reading speed of the readers is mostly because of their ability to move their eyes down towards the page center, whereas, they also incorporate peripheral vision in order to keep capturing all the phrases and words that are lying in the off-center.

Sweep Hands Across the Page

When it is all about speed reading, directing the eyes down and across a page in a specific pattern, rhythm and speed are highly crucial. You can do this by using your own hand as the guiding pointer that will help your eyes in leading them down and across the page. You can also take your hand as an example of a leader dog who is leading a blind person in the street. So, direct your eyes in a way so that they follow your hand, wherever is taking you. Maintenance of the rhythm is also significant as you will be able to increase your reading speed dramatically through time. With the help of this method, you will be able to gain in speed when reading as your reading speed could increase from 10% - 100% depending on how you effective you follow your hand rhythm.

Avoid Skipping Back

We reduce our reading speed slowly because of some skip-backs that involve the reading of sentences and words again and again. The majority of people have this habit, they go back and read again and again as in childhood, they were taught by teachers to re-read the words multiple times when they mispronounced them. As adults they are not verbalizing the words loudly, but rather unconsciously utilize those skip-backs, as they have this strong habit of correcting mispronounced words. By utilizing this method, you will be able to increase your reading speed from 25% - 50%.

Reduce Fixation Time

In the process of reading, most people have the bad habit of staying fixed upon a single word for a large time period. This habit is useful with children who are learning to read and recognize word patterns. Adults though are not supposed to do this and this unfortunate they have this habit that dramatically slows down the process of reading. Next time when you are reading a book, try to find out if you still have this habit of staying fixed in a single word for a long period of time and if yes, then it is important for you to loose this habit. With this method, you will be able to enhance your speed of reading from 10% - 50%.

Don't Move Your Lips

In childhood, we are taught to read each and every word loudly so as for our teacher to hear clearly and immediately correct our mistakes. Just like other reading habits this is acceptable but it would have been better if we were aware of the the language skills needed in the development and growth phase. Somewhere inside, the basic reason behind this teaching method is to continue the word's pronunciation internally or by simply moving the lips while reading. Our eyes are able to identify sentence structures or words faster than saying them loudly, therefore, if you continue to verbalize the words you are reading by moving your lips, your reading speed will drop dramatically. Therefore, if you try not to use your lips nor say the words aloud, you will be able to increase your reading speed from 50% - 250%.

No Need to Read Filler Words

Filler words are completely meaningless and contribute very little in the entire sentence. Such words include 'and', 'the', 'is', 'this', 'that', 'a', 'what' along with other similar words. With continuous practice, you will be able to teach yourself a quick skimming through these words, even when you are not reading them consciously. Therefore, by not reading the fillet words, you will be able to enhance your reading speed from 50% - 100%.

Reading Speed Alternate

As you are moving forward with the guidelines of speed reading, it is essential to take a test by moving yourself out of the comfort zone and this is done by simply challenging yourself about faster reading speed. Everyone has a specific level of comfort to read everything which is equally right and justified. But when we go beyond this level of comfort, our understanding, and comprehension of the information we read changes a lot. Most people are unable to recognize that this change is temporary and the brain will be adjusted in a small time with a new reading speed and comprehension.

Almost every child has an unimpressive skill of reading and their speed is such low that they take even one minute to read one short sentence. But with the passage of time, you become comfortable with this speed as it allows you to grasp and comprehend all the information that you are reading. With time, your reading speed touches the new comfort level that you have today. Nothing can stop you from these transitions from the lower level to the higher level by simply challenging and testing your speed of reading on the daily basis. This method helps people in accelerate their reading speed from 10% - 100%.

Visual Mapping

If you want to be able to understand and comprehend most of the information that you read, it is necessary to make mental visual maps about every paragraph, sentence, chapter and topic during the entire process of reading.

Practice is the Key

 After you have read all the strategies and techniques about accelerating the speed of reading, the key to enhancing the speed is daily practice. By performing a thorough and consistent practice in time, you will able to get your reading speed beyond your present limitations and capabilities.

SQ3R Learning Process

This a simple and easy learning method which will help you in assimilating all the information that you read in an effective and patterned way. This method also requires reading speed and comprehension of the information read.

i. Survey Stage

This survey stage incorporates a complete overview of all the reading material that you are going to learn. At this time, you must be sure that all the necessary resources and tools are present in your hand before moving towards the survey stage.

Start the process by generally having an overview of the material. Take into notice all the topics, keywords, chapters and headings along with the important information that is relevant to the topic.

ii. Question Stage

At this stage, you have to question the material you are going to read, but it should be in such way that enhances your understanding and comprehension regarding the topic.

If you ask deeper questions, you will be able to get your mind prepared for the process of learning.

It doesn't have any importance if you are unable to answer correctly. Only the thing that matters is that when you are opening the mind to all possibilities needed by this question has to be answered, you will be able to move forward with the regime learning.

You must also keep in mind that you are only asking those questions that are not answered by the information available and are important in the understanding of the topic.

iii. Reading Stage

At this stage, it is necessary to spend all the time practicing the reading with speed drawing on the guidelines mentioned above. This also involves the utilization of all the strategies and methods mentioned above.

In the process of speed reading, it is necessary to keep in mind questions that you will be able to answer after reading the material.

iv. Reciting Stage

This reciting stage involves the answering of all the questions along with the organization of the information that you are reading in such a way that it helps you in understanding the topic further.

This review stage is the final stage that will help you in locking the information in long term memory.

You should spend time in reviewing the information you collected while using all the skills and senses to lock all the things for a future recall.

SQ3		
S	**SURVEY**	PREVIEW
Q	**QUESTION**	ASK GUIDE QUESTIONS
R	**READ**	READ FOR MEANING
R	**RECITE**	TEST YOURSELF
R	**REVIEW**	REVIEW AFTER YOU READ

Now it is time to talk about real life situations and setups in which we can apply those speed reading tips and techniques so as to get maximum results. The next chapter will guide you on 'where to apply' speed reading in both personal and professional life.

Where to Apply Speed Reading?

As we saw in the previous chapter, speed reading tips focus on gaining some benefit from the text we read. The objectives of speed reading depend upon the given environment. We need to apply speed reading tips and techniques in professional as well as domestic setup. Speed reading has never been a worthless skill and it never will be. After you have improved your skills of reading, it is easy to apply them everywhere you want. Speed reading is necessary for daily life and it holds great significance when you are a businessman or a student. Such as, in the bundle of emails that you receive each day, you will be able to scrutinize what is the important one if have higher speed reading and this will prevent you from wasting so much time.

High speed reading is important when you are in a business meeting as it will provide you with enough confidence to put your point of view forward. Reading enables you to identify the important facts that can give you knowledge. When you have a high speed reading and you are able to understand each and everything quickly by simply giving it a high reading, this means that you are also enhancing your memory with the increase in the speed. That is why, it is important to have the speed reading in order to understand all the things quickly. High speed is necessary when you have to a large amount of content to read and very little time and it is essential to get a complete and thorough understanding of the material.

People feel less confident more often in some important meeting or conversation because of the lack of reading and writing skills, this is how they are reluctant in performing many different tasks and in turn, they are not producible as they should be. Therefore, it is crucial for such low confident people to increase their speed reading so that they will be able to make their way in their field and they will be able to enhance their performance. You will be able to show everyone what you have in your mind with the clear understanding of all the things because of high speed reading.

High speed enables people to learn more in little time and this is how people who have good reading skills are able to excel compared to the ones' that do not having such skills. With the help of high speed, you will be able to gain more information in a short time as well as improve your memory. You will be able to learn different things by simply reading them. If you have an improved memory, it will be able to lead you in other areas of your life.

If you have a good reading speed, you will be able to identify what is best for you and what article matches your need. This is how your high reading speed will help you overlook the unnecessary information. Therefore, you will be more focused on the topic and your overall efficiency to perform different works will also be enhanced. Speed reading helps you concentrate into a particular chapter.

Silent reading helps you in the comprehension and understanding of all the concepts that are lying in the topic. This will help the readers in getting an overview of all the things that will help them later in all the things, whether they need it at study level or they want to increase their speed for achieving a better position in the business.

One of the most important areas that is highly affected by enhanced reading speed is research. People who are involved in research, have a clear understanding of the importance of the high speed reading. Whenever, research is concerned, people always find it difficult to choose where to start from. Due to the internet, sticking to one particular topic is difficult as you will get a large amount of content online which will make it hard for you to identify which one is the most. After improving your reading skills with the help of high reading speed, you will be able to read a large number of research papers within a small period of time and thus you will be able to select the ones that are most relevant to your needs. This is the ultimate foundation of research if you want to perform the best work.

After getting a clear view of all the things, you will be able to know get access to a large number of material and content so that you can gain as much knowledge as you can while making your research very simple and easy.

When you read many research papers, your knowledge will accumulate and at this time, you should use your high speed skills. You have to identify whether the information provided in the next article is relevant to you or not. This is how you will be able to read more than 100 different research papers in one single day. But before over speeding, it is necessary to have enough information on the back about the topic for which you are finding things. If you have no knowledge, then you will not be able to identify whether the material relates to your topic or not. Therefore, whenever you try high speed reading, make sure that you have enough knowledge to identify which information is helpful for you.

Conclusion

The previous chapter discusses about speed reading in practical life and how it benefits the speed reader to get a cutting edge over others who don't have this skill. Speed reading is one of the highly significant skills that engages the reader's eyes and brain for better understanding. The acceleration of speed reading involves the breaking of unfortunate childhood habits that prevent every reader from reading and understanding effectively. To become a fast reader is not important, but becoming a fast reader with enhanced learning and understanding is.

The development of high speed reading involves the adaptation of various techniques that includes the reading of the words in the form of blocks and chunks and breaking sub-vocalization habit. Whereas, eye movement, regression and lack of concentration are key important factors that contribute to high-speed reading.

Speed reading encompasses various benefits that enable the reader to perform well with more confidence and knowledge. It is not only the speed that is improving but it is also the learning ability and the understanding of various things that is taking place on one side. It enhances the focus of the reader on the particular topic by connecting different concepts to each other, thereby providing a better understanding.

The use of certain tips that increase the speed reading involves the use of a pointer, avoiding of sub-vocalization and over-speeding along with active reading, consistency and eye span. These tips enable the reader to effectively read the context in terms of high speed and better understanding.

To achieve high-speed reading, there are some strategies required in order to accomplish this task: you can use preview if you have too large or lengthy context or you can move to skimming if your data is quite small, clustering can also be performed to optimize the speed reading skills.

There are some generic tips for speed reading that enable the user to learn more effectively, like reading your context in the form of blocks and chunks. This will help you achieve the highest level of speed reading in a fairly short period of time. Eye movement and sentence completion will help the reader in achieving more speed within the short time span.

Therefore, it is necessary to accelerate speed reading if more attention and understanding of the context is required. This is not only helpful for students, but also for businessmen who wish to perform effectively.

www.ingramcontent.com/pod-product-compliance
Lightning Source LLC
Chambersburg PA
CBHW071813170526
45167CB00003B/1290